MW00489722

# Praise for *The Auntie Way*

Michelle Jacob's *The Auntie Way* is a refreshingly poignant account of how aunties of all stripes—family and found, blood related and chosen, those still with us and those watching over us from the other side—impact our lives in both profound and everyday ways. From teaching us to love ourselves in all of our eccentricities and finding value in the mundane to lifting others up and taking strong stands when necessary, Jacob's "auntie magic" provides a road map to "upgrade" every part of who and what we are for ourselves, our families, our communities, and our wider field of relations. Though, as one selection reminds us, there's no such thing as a "perfect" Auntie, I've been fortunate to know many who, by simply taking an interest in my life, have made me a better son, brother, uncle, teacher, mentor, and friend. Reading *The Auntie Way* brought them back to me for a time, reminding me of all they continue to mean to me and all that I continue to owe them in return.

    -Dr. Kirby Brown (Cherokee Nation), Author of *Stoking the Fire: Nationhood in Cherokee Writing, 1907-1970*

Michelle Jacob expands on her groundbreaking Native feminist works *Yakama Rising* and *Indian*

*Pilgrims* to offer a user-friendly workbook on how Native wisdom is shared, how decolonization is practiced and shows us how Auntie love is healing. This book offers Auntie stories as tools to instruct us on ways to love harder, decolonize more fiercely and share wisdom through kindness. Michelle Jacob has given us a set of stories we can go to again and again, and share through generations.

-Dr. Angie Morrill (Klamath Tribes), Director of Indian Education, Portland Public Schools

*The Auntie Way* is such a beautiful gift to the world. Each story reflects an Auntie we may have had growing up, or wish we had, or have been, or wish we could be. The stories, which are both light-hearted and deeply profound, invite us to reflect on and appreciate the Aunties in our lives, and to aspire to their wit, wisdom, and resourcefulness. Through story, reflection, and journaling, Dr. Jacob walks us along a path of remembering and dreaming so that we, as our Aunties often demand (in a good way), can become our best selves.

-Dr. Leilani Sabzalian (Alutiiq), Author of *Indigenous Children's Survivance in Public Schools*

In *The Auntie Way*, we are invited into stories that help us reflect on, appreciate, and learn from the "aunties" in all parts of our lives. Through stories and reflection prompts, the reader has the opportunity to think deeply about the wisdom, support, and guidance they have gotten from mentors ("aunties") as they navigate life. This collection of stories allows us to center the love, wisdom, and power provided to us by "aunties" from our past, present, and future.

-Dr. Anthony B. Craig (Yakama), Director of Leadership for Learning, University of Washington

Dr. Jacob has written a beautiful book of stories demonstrating the need for, and the effects of, love in our lives, particularly from our 'Aunties'. It makes me laugh, cry, smile, and be inspired. This book shows us the importance of love, family, and caring in many forms, and how much we all need Aunties in our lives. Dr. Jacob is one of my Academic Aunties, and now she can be your Auntie too!

-Stephany RunningHawk Johnson (Oglala Lakota), Author of "Native Philosophy as the Basis for Secondary Science Curriculum"

"This beautiful lyrical weaving captures the humor, grace, and responsibility expressed in the very special relationship we aunties and auntie'd have among each other and to ourselves. Dr. Auntie Michelle not only tells the stories of our aunties, she opens and demonstrates for us, giving the auntie nudge, how to practice the auntie way and to be proud of who we are and what we do when Auntie-ing. *The Auntie Way* is proof that auntie stories are good medicine."

-Yvonne P. Sherwood (Spokane/Coeur d'Alene), University of Toronto, Mississauga; Author of "Toward, With, and From a Fourth World"

# The Auntie Way

# ALSO BY MICHELLE M. JACOB

*Yakama Rising: Indigenous Cultural Revitalization, Activism, and Healing*

*Indian Pilgrims: Indigenous Journeys of Activism and Healing with Saint Kateri Tekakwitha*

*On Indian Ground: A Return to Indigenous Knowledge: Generating Hope, Leadership, and Sovereignty Through Education in the Northwest* (co-edited with Stephany RunningHawk Johnson)

# The Auntie Way:
# Stories Celebrating Kindness, Fierceness, and Creativity

Written by:

Michelle M. Jacob

Illustrated by:

Crystal Buck

Published by:

Anahuy Mentoring, LLC

Whitefish, MT

## ANAHUY MENTORING, LLC
EXCELLENCE IN INDIGENOUS METHODS

Author royalties are donated to the Sapsik'ʷałá Program at the University of Oregon to support the next generation of Indigenous teachers. By purchasing this book, you are supporting Indigenous self-determination in education. Kw'alanúushamash! (I am grateful to you!)

ISBN (paperback): 978-1-7346151-0-4
ISBN (e-book): 978-1-7346151-1-1

Cover design by Christopher J. Andersen
Cover illustration by Crystal Buck

Library of Congress Control Number:
2020904096

Copyright © 2020 Anahuy Mentoring, LLC
Whitefish, MT

http://www.anahuymentoring.com
http://www.auntieway.com

All rights reserved. This book, or parts thereof, may not be reproduced in any form without permission.

This book is dedicated to all Aunties
who bring their kindness, fierceness, and
creativity to the world.

# Table of Contents

# Introduction

In the stories that follow, you will learn about the power and wisdom of what I am calling "The Auntie Way." I see The Auntie Way as an important methodology about listening, guiding, and helping. Aunties may or may not be "blood relatives" and in the stories that follow I write about a variety of Aunties, all who provide powerful examples of ways of being in the world. They are experts in "Auntie-ing," a verb I made up that I find to be both fun and important, much as Aunties are. I see The Auntie Way as an important contribution to anyone seeking to be a teacher or leader. I wish all of our organizations, institutions, families, and relationships were saturated with the love and care that is the foundation for The Auntie Way.

What is The Auntie Way? You can decide for yourself, as you read the brief stories that follow. You bring your own experiences and wisdom and perspectives to these stories, and to your life. I cannot tell you what The Auntie Way is or should be for you. But I hope that how I describe Auntie-ing is helpful for you. For me, The Auntie Way is the very best of what I see my Aunties over the years giving to me, to help me find the strength and courage to be my best self—or at least to try. And the understanding and patience to know that it is ok to fail. That failure is part of learning and growing; it expands our ability to love and care, if we allow it.

Some readers will perhaps want to know if the stories in this book are true with a capital T. I will say this: these stories are *inspired* by actual events, but are not a literal and exact documentation of everything I've witnessed. For example, I have never seen a *real* fire-breathing dragon at the university. Thus, the stories are more like little bits of creative nonfiction for you to taste and, I hope, enjoy.

I include journaling and discussion questions after each story, as a way to help encourage deeper engagement with the lessons and ideas in the stories. I hope the questions will also prompt you to more deeply engage your own inner wisdom. The questions can be utilized by readers either individually or in a group, depending on whether you are reading the book by yourself or as part of a collective. I am a scholar by training, so I cannot help but include notes and definitions here and there, but I've tried to minimize these so as not to interrupt the flow of the book.

In my family, and in my life, Aunties are precious and treasured. I believe Auntie-ing has something powerful and important to teach all of us. The lessons stem from women's lives, and all genders can learn from The Auntie Way. I hope these stories help reflect back to you the precious treasures in your life and in yourself.

# Auntie Love

I'm excited about a book of stories of Auntie-ing and Auntie Love.

Why?

Because Aunties are *awesome*.

Aunties can do *anything*.

Aunties can make your sides hurt from deep, shaking, almost-wetting-your-pants-laughter.

Aunties can soothe your sorrows.

Aunties can sit quietly and listen, just when you thought the whole world had gone mad and no one would ever listen to your voice again.

Aunties can kick your butt into gear when you procrastinate for too long. Not because they are overly concerned with to-do lists getting done, although that *may* be a secret joy of theirs. *Rather,* they see how your procrastinating prevents us from seeing your best self.

Aunties have a knack for knowing *just* when it's the right time for ice cream. She'll get strawberry. What will you have today?

Aunties will let you upgrade to a waffle cone.

Aunties, through their love and strength and example, keep reminding you: your *whole life* can be an upgrade to a waffle cone, if you want.

Aunties are *awesome*.

# Journaling and Discussion Questions for "Auntie Love"

1. When is the last time that you laughed a big, deep belly laugh with someone? Who were you with and what were you laughing about?

2. Share a brief story about someone who has helped you see you could be more, or do more, in a way that really helped you become the person you wanted to be. What did they do or say? What were you able to overcome or accomplish because of their help?

3. "Auntie Love" proposes the possibility of your whole life being like "an upgrade to a waffle cone." What might this look like for you? Please brainstorm and describe your dream life. Not just an "ok" life, or a "basic" life, but the BEST possible life you can imagine for yourself—one which

seems like a fun treat you are fortunate to have, every single day. Write some notes to yourself to remind you of your dream. Better yet, write yourself a letter explaining your dream. Find an envelope and stamp and mail it to yourself!

# Auntie in Our Planner

One day, I was cleaning out a box of precious belongings, you know the kind of box, a pretty little thing you put this and that into over the days, weeks, months, years.

Until you don't.

And then you kind of forget about it in the hustle and bustle of everyday life. Until one day you unexpectedly come across it. I'd forgotten how pretty this box is. I opened the lid. What treasures awaited me?

Sparkly stickers: rainbows, teddy bears, stars, smiley faces. Cute little erasers in the shape of a basketball, a panda, a unicorn head. Postcards and mementos from travels with loved ones; I used to be *fascinated* with those flattened penny souvenir machines. Small wallet-sized photos. You know, from the time when people used to carry plastic sleeves of photos inside their wallets.

I flipped through the photos, moving quickly through the stack. And there she was. Auntie.

I smiled.

A great big smile, the kind of smile that takes up your whole face.

Tears moistened my eyes. I was *so happy* to see that photo. To see her.

My Auntie was delicate and graceful. Petite. And fiercely stubborn.

She was soft-spoken. Until she wasn't.

I *adored* her.

I love that particular photo *so* much. You know how sometimes photos only *kind of* look like a person—like some gremlin got into the Photo Haus darkroom and changed the image so it is only a mere approximation of the person in the portrait? Well this photo did not fall victim to gremlin intervention. I love the photo because of its spot-on representation of Auntie. It *is* her.

An 80s era studio portrait. Her hands gracefully poised by her brown face, dignified with wrinkles here and there. Her hair, surely just out of the beauty parlor, permed and set and sprayed in perfect form. Her glasses, oversized, with a dark tint. Her clothes, impeccably ironed.

When I gaze at her picture, I see one of my *favorite* forms of Native American feminine beauty. A mix of pool hall tavern toughness from the reservation back home, and savvy adaptation of Southern California fashion and trappings. I can hear her voice on the telephone, greeting my dad in our Indigenous language, me listening in on the other line in the kitchen.

I love my Auntie *so* much. Always have. Always will.

That day, with my huge smile hurting my face and tears choking me up, phlegm thick in my throat— almost as thick as my happy memories, I put the photo in the plastic pocket inside the cover of my planner. From there, Auntie watched over me as I wrote my appointments into the planner, dutifully filling the squares of time.

Auntie came with me to work, helped me through boring meetings, difficult emails, and personal dilemmas. When I felt lost in the busy-ness of the day, or annoyed by an outlandish request being made of me, I had only to take a peek inside my planner to find strength and reassurance.

We might all need an Auntie in the inside pocket of our planner.

# Journaling and Discussion Questions for "Auntie in Our Planner"

1. Think about a little memento box from your past, whether real or imagined. What might be inside of it? What meaning do these objects have for you, either in the past and/or now?

2. Whose wallet-sized photo would you be delighted to find in your memento box? Why?

3. If, far into the future, a young person found a photo of you in their memento box, what would you want them to remember about you? How would you want their memories of you to guide them in their life?

# Writing Group Prompt

Writing can be a solitary endeavor. Without community, writers can become alienated from their surroundings, even from themselves. So I saw a flyer for a writer's group in town and I showed up. The first week I tried to go they cancelled the group meeting, as there was a competing art event happening in the same space. How lovely! But also, perhaps, an excuse for me to not show up the following week. Instead, I heard the whisper of my Auntie encouraging me to attend, and so I went. At the end of the group meeting, which was filled with fun prompts and freewriting, and generous and supportive comments, one of the writers gave the group a prompt to use as homework, should we so choose. The prompt: **Define what art is.**

\*       \*       \*

Art is everything. Art is nothing.

Art is the scribbles of color my niece made on a yellow pad of paper one day, which she left behind at my house on our reservation, content her drawing had fulfilled its truth and duty and purpose in the few minutes it took her six-year-old hands to make. The gift, as always, happened in the present for my young niece, a wise artist who seeks and finds her joy in the simplicity of making. She shows me the purity and love involved in creation; how simple this complex lesson can be. It is a joy; instant, and eternal, all at once.

Art is the curves and lines and colors and shapes I saw hanging on the wall in Antibes at the Picasso Museum perched above the Mediterranean. I feasted my eyes on the many drafts of drawings on display. To me, those rough sketches were the masterpieces, his drawing a simple fish over and over, again and again as he played with form and texture, size, shape, and perspective. A joyous and disciplined play, I think; instant and eternal, draft and masterpiece, all at once.

I write these words on a chilly December morning in Northwest Montana, thinking of those charcoal fish who whispered to me in Southern France on a warm late-summer day, "The magic is in the practice. The freedom is in the discipline."

Back in Montana, I pause, look up from the page and see the masterpiece framed and displayed in a place of honor above the mantel. It is perhaps my favorite work of art in the whole world. I see genius in the colors and lines and shapes, on that seemingly ordinary piece of yellow lined paper. Next week we'll celebrate the artist's 19th birthday.

I was half right: Art is everything.

# Journaling and Discussion Questions for "Writing Group Prompt"

1. Briefly describe a time when you felt lonely or isolated, and how you got through that time. What is an image you can keep in mind, or an object you can look at (such as the child's artwork on the mantle in "Writing Group Prompt"), to remind yourself you're not alone?

2. In "Writing Group Prompt," the young niece is celebrated for her "genius" in "scribbles of color" on a piece of notebook paper. Think of someone you love, for whom you would be happy and proud of their work, no matter the result. How do you show that respect and love, whether in big ways or small?

3. Describe two things that are similar, but one is widely thought of as fancy and one is widely

thought of as ordinary. Might you ever prefer the ordinary over the fancy? Why or why not?

# Auntie's Quilt

Whenever I feel a chill, either from the air or from within, I am comforted by my Auntie's quilt she made for me. I can see her in my memory, down on all fours on the basement floor, carefully laying out the pieces, her masterpiece. Such care and precision with those little squares she would sew together in perfect order, tight straight stiches surrounding those blocks of fabric. The stiches like little soldiers instructed by General Auntie to always watch over me, keep me safe and warm.

After sewing the blocks, Auntie would diverge from the straight tight rows of stitching; she would do dreamy curvy stiches by hand when she quilted all the layers together; layers of warmth and love, trust, kindness, generosity into each pull of the needle through the fabric and batting. I delighted in watching her make those curvy lines of stiches; they were magical, like the Olympic rhythmic gymnasts I enjoyed seeing on tv when they danced with that long, flowy ribbon. Auntie bought me one of those ribbons one year and I danced that ribbon through the yard; over the lawn, on the driveway, to complete my own quilted pattern of movement.

Auntie used pink and purple stiches on my quilt, my favorite colors. I remember as a child being sick more often than not and sentenced to bed rest, horrible for a child who would rather be ribbon dancing outside. I'd pull that quilt up to my chin to keep the chills away. With my hands, almost always icy cold, I'd trace the curvy stiches, which looked a bit like jigsaw puzzle pieces, and I'd puzzle over things: When would I heal? Would I have to go back to the Indian Health Service clinic? If so, would the nice grandfatherly doctor be in? Or the one who I was certain was a dangerous person who harmed little girls? I remember crying one time when that man, the bad doctor, said what he wanted to do to investigate my pain. I cried and made everyone feel awkward and we left the clinic with a bottle of prescribed generic Tylenol; they always sent us home with that, like there was some kind of incentive program to get rid of it. Or maybe that was all they had.

Back at home, safe under Auntie's quilt, I would caress those jigsaw puzzle stiches, smoothing them, their curvy shapes, feeling the batting underneath the curvy lines and the soldier stitched squares. My Auntie's smell, a mix of fabric softener and Tabu perfume, lingered on the quilt. Even now, decades later, I remember that scent and the lingering aroma of black coffee, which she always had warming in a pot, perpetual cup nearby. I remember the feel of her hair sprayed, permed hair touching my cheek. I think back to that quilt, how soft it was, while also being remarkably tough armor. Even when General Auntie wasn't around, I always had her legions of soldiers, the rows of stiches in my quilt, watching over me, getting me through the battles of illness and fear, urging me to be a ribbon dancer of life.

# Journaling and Discussion Questions for "Auntie's Quilt"

1. Describe the smell you associate with someone you love and who helped you feel safe when you were younger. What is a memory you have of that person and that smell?

2. What is something you puzzled over when you were younger? Where did you do your puzzling?

3. If you were to design a quilt to help show your love and caring for a young person, what colors and designs of fabric might you include? Would the stiches be in a special pattern? Describe the meaning of each of your creative choices. How might such a quilt help you feel safe, too?

# Chez Auntie

Bake at 400 degrees Fahrenheit for 20-22 minutes or until the cheese in the center is melted and the edges are browned.

Some Aunties are brilliant homemakers, childcare providers, and cooks. Some are so talented in the kitchen that they can *actually* be called chefs.

I can see the bistro now, at the only strip mall on the rez: Chez Auntie.

I love it. I'd eat there everyday if I could.

But what about the Aunties who are juggling school and work. Elder care. The laundry machine broke and there are no quarters for the laundromat. The dog just peed on the floor. No, not the carpet. Thank God! But would anyone really notice a pee stain on your carpet? It's so bad already. All worn down with the greyish matted path that shows you where everyone walks, like ruts on the slow lane of Highway 97.

What about *these* Aunties?

What goes on in their kitchen when the big yellow school bus arrives at the end of the driveway and the kids pile off, backpacks and shoelaces dragging as they shuffle into the house?

The oven dial clicks to Bake. Temperature set to 400. A frozen pizza is ceremoniously removed from the freezer. The oldest nephew reads the instructions off the box while Auntie uses scissors to cut the plastic away from the disk-shaped comfort food. We put the pizza into the oven. Set the timer. Yes, it's ok that the oven clock gets messed up when you push the timer button in and spin it to 20 minutes.

The old oven clock numbers flip, like the train schedule display board in European train stations; we saw them in the movies.

Click, flip, click, flip. Amsterdam! Paris! Rome! Where shall we go?!

We can go *anywhere* in this sacred 20 minutes of happiness and hope.

Young people and Auntie traveling around the world, awaiting a frozen pizza. We always know when the cheese is melted and the crust is golden brown, and our journey ends just in time. Grab the red pepper flakes.

Chez Auntie indeed.

Note: Chez (pronounced "shey" like the beginning of the word "shade") is a French word that is often translated as "at the home of" or "in the manner of" and is sometimes used in restaurant names; for example, Chez Michelle could be the name of a bistro if I opened one in Wapato, which I will not, because I'm pretty sure folks can bake their own frozen pizzas.

# Journaling and Discussion Questions for "Chez Auntie"

1. Name someone you know, whose company and way of being is really fun to be around, and if they opened a restaurant, you'd want to eat there as often as you could. What about this person makes you want to be around them so much?

2. Who is someone you admire who may have limited resources but accomplishes wonderful things or shows a spirit of generosity? Describe how they go about accomplishing things or being generous.

3. Describe one of your comfort foods. With whom do you associate it? What is a fond memory of that person?

# Petticoats and Whispers

I remember when Elizabeth Cady Stanton came to my school on the reservation.

She was elegant.

All good posture with a fancy dress.

You could tell her dress was custom made, tailored carefully stich by stich, with a gazillion black cloth covered buttons and those tiny pieces of elastic that are loops, into which the buttons barely fit. What patience to fasten all of those each time one got dressed!

All prim and proper, real old timey stuff.

The whole dress was black. Practical I think, for raising hell in her upper-class way, urging men to acknowledge and honor women as real human beings.

I could image her tromping around 1800s upstate New York, boots and petticoats weaving through the streets, dodging the oncoming horses and carriages.

She came all the way across Turtle Island to visit our school, traveling across the continent and through time—more decades than a century.

Her outfit was lovingly and painstakingly sewn by Auntie, who had consulted the big pattern catalogs at all the fabric stores. You know the ones, those monstrous books at the tables and chairs, where you gaze at the colorful drawings and trendy models, and pick out the pattern you want, and then go to the massive file cabinets to get the real deal—make sure you select the correct size.

Then on to fabric, notions, the fabric cutting station, and finally the cashier.

Oh, the hours and hours we'd spend at the fabric stores.

Auntie could spend all day, every day, there.

But for Elizabeth Cady Stanton, the pattern catalog books at the fabric stores were not sufficient. Her dress required more research.

Auntie went to the local libraries, historical societies, museums, finding anything she could about suffragists and carefully examining their clothes.

Auntie poured over the files, books, microfilm of old newspapers. She took notes. She weaved together an image of what she wanted to make. She created her own patterns for each component of the dress.

A lot of love and care went into that dress. The dress itself an expression of Auntie Love. The dress conveyed women's brilliance and power, and yes, the literal message of women's empowerment and the 19th amendment in my speech for a project at the public school on my reservation.

Stand straight!

Tall posture, like Auntie taught.

Do you hear that sound? It might be the whisper of my petticoat.

Or maybe it's the whisper of generations of Aunties loving their nieces.

# Journaling and Discussion Questions for "Petticoats and Whispers"

1. Describe your own posture and what you think it says about you. Who is someone you think of as having good posture? Describe this person and their posture.

2. If you could bring a historical figure across time and place to visit with you and your peers, who's one person you'd choose? Why?

3. Think of someone you have known who was "old-fashioned." Describe this person—their dress, their manner. What did you perhaps think of them when you were younger and how might your thoughts be different now?

# I Auntie'd Myself Today

I Auntie'd myself today.

I was feeling tired and stressed and sad and lonely.

For no reason at all. And for every *possible* reason.

I got myself a cup of coffee choosing the prettiest mug I saw and, as is my fashion, I filled it full to the brim.

I brushed crumbs off the table and sat down. I paid attention to the sounds and textures around me. I see the lines on the floor, some now confettied with crumbs I'd brushed aside. I hear the neighbor's dishwasher humming through the wall. I notice the glow of the lights overhead, that soft yellow light almost like fire. How pretty and warm the light feels.

The smell of coffee freshly ground and brewed, a smell so deep and rich it envelops me. I'm a pea in the pod of the coffee aroma. It keeps me safe. It slows me down. It shelters me, cradles me. I'm bundled up in the babyboard of coffee. I'm bound and safe and small—and I'm opened up to a wide expansive vista, all at once.

It reminds me of when I was younger and riding along with my Auntie in her *big* car with power windows I *yearned* to play with. Up down, up, down.

Instead, I brush the cloth on the seat. Thank God this was the era before car seats. I sat regally, up front in the passenger seat, like a real adult. I brushed the cloth seat with my hand; it felt like velvet.

Back and forth I'd rub the grain and it magically would change colors. Tan. Brown. Now tan again, like the fur coats deer wear as they walk the runway in the forest, color changing with the seasons.

As I sat there, copilot of Captain Auntie's magic vessel, I knew in my little heart that anything is possible.

On these precious and magical journeys, I'd go with Auntie to the yarn shop, the fabric store or, on special occasions, to the toy store.

"Pick something out, and make sure it is something your mother wouldn't let you choose," she'd say in her elegant and soft voice, a mischievous sparkle in her dark brown eyes.

That's how Rub A Dub Doggie came into my life.

I remember removing him from his packaging and I held him in my lap on the way home. My first dog!

We recounted the story at home, telling my mother the instructions and permission Auntie had given at the toy store in the Yakima Mall for me to choose something that might be ridiculous.

"So *what* did you get?" Mom asked, pretending to be exasperated.

I revealed Rub A Dub Doggie and said his name with the joy and enthusiasm of a winner down at the Bingo Hall.

Mom took him into her hands and said, "You're right. I *wouldn't* let you choose a plastic dog to take a bath with! For goodness sake!"

She gave him back and shook her head in pretend disappointment.

"Yes, but he has soft ears and when they're wet, I can move the handle on his neck so he can shake his ears dry! Look!"

Rub A Dub Doggie, like real dogs, was a good listener and companion.

In my mind's eye I can imagine him sitting with me now, his big brown puppy eyes watching over me while I write.

I imagine Auntie here, too, clicking away with her knitting needles, working on her next project, a cable knit sweater to keep me warm.

Auntie and Rub A Dub Doggie are sitting beside me, urging me to keep writing, keep creating with the joy of a little girl being amazed at the changing grain and color of fabric.

I sip the last of my coffee from the cobalt blue mug, the ceramic still warm from the hot liquid, much as my heart is still warm with memories of Auntie.

I'm so glad I Auntie'd myself today.

# Journaling and Discussion Questions for "I Auntie'd Myself Today"

1. In this story, Auntie-ing is described as a way of expressing care and love; it leaves our heart feeling warm with good memories. What would "Auntie-ing" yourself mean, to you?

2. Who is someone you associate with these Auntie traits: fun, care, and concern? Describe a time when that person exhibited these traits.

3. What is one way you can "Auntie" yourself today?

# I Love Pyaxí* (Bitterroot)

I love pyaxí.

She's bitter and strong and difficult and beautiful.

She's grounded—fierce.

She makes you kneel. Or stoop.

She thrives where pretty much no one else will.

She makes you pay attention.

She's holy.

She teaches us the power of the collective.

Literally.

Folks, have you ever tried to dig and peel an entire gunnysack of pyaxí by yourself?

Yeah. You're way better off filling a station wagon full of people to come help you. It doesn't really matter who. Anyone willing to learn and help makes for good company.

Pyaxí teaches us this, too.

By the time we stop for gas, wind our way up the ridge, and bounce down that rutted, rocky road, we're all so grateful to be there.

The petty annoyances—the sibling squabbles, the long-held grudges, the arguments about who ate too much garlic last night or too many sunflower seeds this morning—that all just drifts away.

I think the brisk spring wind took it.

So grab a kápin (digging tool) and breathe in that fresh spring air!

Enjoy the sunny morning—that gorgeous contrast of the biscuit-colored Earth meeting the blue, blue Sky.

Literally.

I went to Home Depot and looked at their paint chips. The exact shade is called "Sky Blue."

I never tire of that view. The golden colored earth meeting the crisp blue sky.

I remember Auntie helping teach us to dig; her scarf tied neatly on her head while she prayed to Creator and blessed us before we dug our first roots.

Often when we dig pyax̱í we can see the dip of Status Pass in the distance. We have fond memories of journeys taken that way, and great hopes for future fun to be had.

That's the way to Nch'i Wána, the Big River (Columbia River), and to Portland with its tax-free shopping malls, Trail Blazer basketball games, and the steakhouse my dad sometimes treats my nephews to—a place with all you can eat meat, can you imagine?

On a pyax̱í digging day there is no time for such things. We are alive and at peace with ourselves, each other, and all the world. Even after all these years, Auntie's blessings remain intact. We renew them, and I believe the wind carries our prayers back to her spirit.

I love pya<u>x</u>í.

*Note: Pya<u>x</u>í is the Yakama/Ichishkíin word for bitterroot, a sacred food and dietary staple for many Indigenous peoples, including Yakamas; pya<u>x</u>í continues to be gathered each spring in the traditional way. Pya<u>x</u>í only grows in very rocky soil and it takes practice to learn how to carefully dig the roots without ripping off the top of the plant (which leaves the gatherer without any food). To hear our Elder, Dr. Virginia Beavert, pronounce pya<u>x</u>í, please refer to the audio files from her Yakama Ichishkíin dictionary: <u>http://depts.washington.edu/sahaptin/Sahdic.h</u> <u>tm</u>

(I share more about the dictionary and Dr. Beavert at the end of the last story in this book.) For those readers who are in a hurry or do not have internet access right now, I'll share with you that English speakers would likely pronounce pya<u>x</u>í as: pee-ya-XHEE.

# Journaling and Discussion Questions for "I Love Pyax̱í"

1. Describe the "personality" of one of your favorite plants. What are the characteristics of the plant that you enjoy or respect most?

2. Discuss a time when you no longer were bothered by "petty annoyances." What contributed to your feeling of peace?

3. Think about a task or project that could not be accomplished without a collective. What joys and challenges did each member of the collective bring? How did you grow as a person, and in your relationships, through that experience?

# Super Auntie Sue

Sometimes Aunties have it within them to Auntie an entire school. This is a rare sort of Auntie, one who has a big heart, big patience, a love for laughter. She obviously has super powers, including the ability to listen to the mumbling words and awkward shame and fleeting hope of hundreds of middle schoolers.

Have you seen such an Auntie?

Have you *had* such an Auntie?

If so, you're blessed. I know I am.

Attending public school on my reservation, I never had a Native American classroom teacher. Our district had simply not hired any. For those of us who made it through grades K-5 and on to middle school, we had, for three glorious years, perhaps when we needed it most, but of course were not aware of it—because hello! We were *middle schoolers*—we had Super Auntie Sue.

Super Auntie Sue was one of the counselors at our middle school. Her office was our refuge. We would go there to sit. To talk. To be. That's the thing about Aunties. They know when to listen. When to speak. When to guide. When to nudge. And when to do a good old-fashioned shove, like being shoved out of the way of an oncoming car, except in this case you are also driving the car to a bad decision.

When to tell you about the proud history of our people and when to demand that you go out and make a better future for us. Don't you see? She might tell you, again:

Your actions and behaviors represent *our people*.

Everything you do *matters*.

*You are important.*

Aunties can give the most supportive, nurturing butt kicking you ever saw. Super Aunties have a way of telling you to pull yourself together, and also affirming it is ok to sometimes completely unravel. Sometimes she can do all of this without even saying a word.

Super Auntie Sue never taught me in the classroom, but she always gave the most demanding homework: Listen to your father. Be kind to your mother. Encourage your friends to come to school. Stop gossiping and being cliquey. Sue gave assignments that were for the *long haul.*

I never received a quarterly or midterm grade from Sue. But I always knew where I stood with her. I think back now, about Sue's long career at the public school, thousands of children needing her attention and love. And she always came through. We always tried our best on Sue's homework because she not only assigned it, she lived it.

She reflected back to us the best in ourselves.

Super Auntie Sue shared with each child her superpowers.

And taught us that we have them, too.

Note: The wonderful work of Sue and the Wapato Indian Club are further discussed in my book, *Yakama Rising.*

# Journaling and Discussion Questions for "Super Auntie Sue"

1. Who is one specific person you know who seems to have superpowers—an extraordinary ability to do something that helps people? Describe them and their superpower.

2. Describe someone who helped you see you have more potential than you originally thought. What did they teach you, and how? How might you share this gift with someone else? Think of someone you see potential in and plan a way to encourage that person.

3. What is a message you'd like to share with a person you wrote about in the previous two questions? Write a thank you note and include your message. Send it to the person (or one of their close friends or relatives) if you can. Even if you

can't send it, please still write the thank you note. The gratitude you express is a gift…to yourself.

# Sandbag and Cookie

So far I've written about Auntie love and the kindness and care and humor that fills us with love and hope. What about when Aunties show love in times of deep confusion and pain? What about when Aunties show love when Uncles betray? Or when an Auntie protects an Uncle who harms?

This topic makes me uncomfortable:

A discomfort like a heavy sandbag pulling on my heart. A discomfort different than being shoulder to sweaty shoulder with strangers in Times Square on a muggy August afternoon, when I hustled from crowded sidewalk to crowded sidewalk, smells of garbage and perspiration oozing up from the streets as I dodged cars, trucks, taxis, strollers, bulging shopping bags on the arms of tourists, the sudden stops of selfie-takers.

Why would I subject myself to this chaos?

To get to Junior's, of course.

Doing battle in midtown, I finally reached my destination. I breathed a sigh of relief and relaxed my shoulders that had creeped up towards my ears with stress, tension, and hypervigilance. The energy of midtown had seeped into my body.

Now, safely and successfully arrived at Junior's, I took comfort in the small lobby-sized café gift shop and its smell of freshly brewed coffee. The cheerfulness of that bright orange color, the restaurant's signature color; it reminds me of the curtains that stand vigilant behind my parents' kitchen table. I feel a moment of calm.

But I also cannot shake that nagging feeling of dread, like the heaviness of a sandbag pulling on my heart. It weighs me down, dampens my spirit, even as I'm surrounded by the comforting smells of sweet treats from the bakery, the upbeat music—Dione Warwick melodically reassuring she's saying a little prayer for me; brightly colored orange joy enveloping us, upbeat young people, impeccably groomed in their starched white uniforms, orange and white paper hats perched atop their heads, the promise of Americana on display. Even amidst this cheerful wonder, the sandbag weighs me down.

I think about my Uncle as a young man. So full of hope, promise and love. How he brought such joy and wonderful stories into my parents' home. The laughter, teasing and merriment surely soaking into the orange curtains, helping to saturate them; storing up the happiness to help us through the hard times we didn't know were coming.

The cleanly shaven young man behind the counter at Junior's wants to know how he can help me. "One Black and White cookie, please." I pay for the cookie and leave—back in the streets to do battle with the crowds and noise, heat and humidity. I make my way up Broadway and see the edge of Central Park. Christopher Columbus watches over the area. I glance up at his statue and feel the strains of a tension headache forming. Seeing the colonizing explorer further dampens my mood.

I cross 59th and make my way into the park. There's a small band playing Beach Boys songs. They have no singer, but I know the words to

"Sloop John B," memorized from the long car trips made with my dad when I was young. I remember when he removed the old radio and had a cassette tape player installed into the car. Afterwards we went to Budget Tapes & Records in Yakima. He got a special brief case looking bag to hold his new cassettes. He filled the case with treasures from Budget and Fred Meyer. Sometimes I was allowed to be our DJ. I felt so special and official with that tan briefcase in my lap, sitting up front in the passenger seat like a boss, whose feet could barely reach the floor mat. I'd sometimes play the sing-songy tunes of the Beach Boys..."Let me go home...I want to go home...Hoist up the John B sail..."

The band announced they'd go on break and thanked the audience. Children, tourists with fanny packs, and I all put money in their open guitar case, and most people clapped. The musicians sipped water and chatted with some audience members. I sat on a newly vacated green-slatted park bench. I took my backpack off and fluffed my shirt to get some air and help me cool off. I removed the orange and white Junior's paper bag from my backpack. I took out the cellophane-wrapped cookie, smiling at the circle of comfort I held in my hands. Sure, there were delis closer by that sell them, but there are none as good, as soft, as perfectly balanced— richness and sweetness all in one—as a Junior's Black and White cookie.

I held the treasure in my hands.

My thoughts returned to Uncle. How could he? Uncle had never harmed me, personally, I told myself. Sure, he'd be a jerk, sometimes showing arrogance. Puffing himself up like a 1970s AIM leader who forgot his manners around women and girls; male chauvinism and homophobia mistaken for "culture," sometimes telling jokes at the expense of our two-spirit relations. Yes, I'd seen and heard that side of Uncle, when my parents were out of ear and eye range. When he used that degrading mode of communication around me, I tried to shut it down, reminding him he could communicate respectfully or move along. Standing toe to toe with Uncle wasn't fun, but I'd been taught not to flinch when someone's being an as*hole. Call them out, tell them how to make it right, and invite them to move along if they don't like it.

But Uncle had no particular power over me. What about the other young people he bullied, belittled, bossed around? Coerced? Touched?

Uncle was a guide, a mentor, a teacher, to many. For a time, he was wonderful at all of these.

But then I heard the rumors. Later I heard testimonies from survivors, hushed and quiet, full of pain and shame.

It's frowned upon to talk about him now; he's been banished—his name and photo erased, the hard work of Aunties to keep us safe. Except for one Auntie, who inexplicably still loves him, and is leading the charge for him to be canonized—St. Uncle who is not even dead yet.

As I sit on the green park bench and hold that cookie in my hand I see the sharp line of division— the black and white frosting clinging to their separate sides.

Uncle's behavior created similar divisions for us. The brave young people who spoke up, dividing themselves from him and his supporters. They even had to divide themselves from their own hope and joy and feeling of safety. He took that from them. The pressures in our family and community to support one another, fracturing in a million different ways. We were all cut on those jagged shards; I think there are still some slivers in my hands. Calluses have grown over them, but at times I still feel and see them.

The band is back from break. A woman vocalist has joined them and is setting up her mic stand. They start their next set, staying with popular oldies tunes. The guitarist plucks out a familiar melody. The small crowd sings along, multiple accents join in the chorus: "Come on, people now, smile on your brother. Everybody get together, try to love one another right now."

I listen to the beautiful choir of voices; see the children dancing, dogs eagerly searching for crumbs on the ground with tails wagging in delight, mothers holding babies and swaying to the music.

I eat the edges of the cookie, the white side and its sweetness balanced by the cakey cookie; the dark side a rich chocolately frosting that makes me crave coffee on this hot day.

I get to the middle part, the division between dark and light. I think about the pain Uncle has caused. And the more distant joy he's brought to our lives and the world, so long ago I'm not sure if it's even still real.

I haven't seen or talked to Uncle for several years. I feel the weight of that sandbag on my heart and my eyes fill with tears.

That damn beautiful sight and sound of the global chorus in front of me: "Come on, people now, smile on your brother. Everybody get together, try to love one another right now."

I feel a rip in the sandbag of sorrow and hate. Is this the path to letting go? To forgiveness? Perhaps. The sand is free now to circulate all throughout my body.

I finish my cookie, wipe my fingers on the Junior's napkin, put another dollar in the guitar case and move along.

Maybe, just for today, Uncle is forgiven.

But for the sake of the all the future generations of nephews and nieces, I will never forget.

# Journaling and Discussion Questions for "Sandbag and Cookie"

1. Describe a time when you felt a heavy weight on your heart due to someone else's behavior. Why did it weigh you down? Did you find it challenging to speak up about the pain the other person was causing? What gave you courage to do so? Or what might give you courage in the future?

2. If you were able to forgive (if not forget) the harmful behavior you wrote about in the previous question, describe the feeling that forgiveness brought to you. If you were not yet able to forgive, what might it take for you to move in that direction? Imagine your "sandbag of sorrow and hate" ripping and releasing your pain, and describe how that release might benefit you.

3. Inevitably, we also harm other people, whether intentionally or unintentionally. Describe an occurrence when you caused someone harm. Next, write a note of apology to a person you've harmed and ask forgiveness. It can be short and sweet (i.e. "I'm sorry my behavior harmed you. Please forgive me."). Or it can be lengthier if you choose. If you wish, send the note to that person. If that is not possible, or if it seems inappropriate in some way, then burn the note or tear it up into a bunch of pieces—while you burn or tear it, (or immediately after you send the note) release the remaining bad feelings you may have about this harm, and embrace the gift of humility in your life.

# Academic Aunties

There's a special group of women who know the secret passages, trap doors, and quick sand of the ivory tower. These women, sometimes elderly, sometimes young, sometimes in between, are good listeners, good observers. They are masterful at choosing their moments, knowing just when to draw a short dagger from the beaded holster at the back of their belt, and thrust it forward to slay a dragon. I've seen it more than once. How can that short little blade do so much for so many?

But these women are not looking for a fight. In general, they are happiest to visit quietly with a small group of people.

They carry themselves in a way that *shows* you who they are. Proud, yet humble. Kind, but will hold you to high standards. These women are tough. Yet velvety soft.

They are Academic Aunties.

Being with them is like attending a calm and rejuvenating tea party. Their care and concern for you is evident in the warm scones they place on the table inside the cloth-lined basket. Did you want jam with your scone? Strawberry or blackberry? Oh! She remembers she has a jar of huckleberry jam she was saving just for this occasion. What wonderful nourishment, in more ways than one.

Academic Aunties tell stories, softly chuckle at jokes, or if naughty jokes are shared sometimes they howl with laughter, passers-by in the hallway peering in with quizzical looks on their faces.

Academic Aunties talk about work projects and their families. They tell stories about back home, share ideas with generosity, and always keep an eye towards helping connect you to what will help you to heal, to be your best you.

Against all odds, these women exist in the halls of academia, a place that is typically hostile to everything Academic Aunties bring: love, kindness, encouragement, patience, hope. So, our Aunties, when needed, keep these magical gifts tucked away. That's why they have such big purses and strong shoulders, from carrying that big bag of Auntie magic.

I've had so many Academic Aunties. At every college I attended, I found at least one.

These women, who have very little to no reason to spend their time and energy, help and hope on you, but in some blessed way see a glint of potential amidst your weary, flunking, lost my scholarship, on academic probation self.

And so, they open their bag of Auntie magic.

They know which form to fill out, and which office to take it to, and which office worker is the least passive aggressive—all of these things that are crucial to stop the bleeding and hemorrhaging of your academic and professional future from fading away.

Academic Aunties are partners in your dreams.

They respect you enough to remind you, in ways both implicit and explicit, that in accepting Auntie help, you become responsible for helping others in the future. You are expected to watch and learn about the Auntie magic in their bags, and to use what you learn to help others struggling with the same quick sand problems that you once fell into, and avoid the trap doors that you once were stumbling over.

I've never seen a job ad for an Academic Auntie. Yet, I cannot imagine living without them. Perhaps it is for the best that HR isn't classifying, reviewing, and ranking one's Academic Auntieness. But maybe it's not. I don't know.

All I know is that Academic Aunties are magical and fierce and kind and patient and creative and demanding—all in a good way. I dream of an academy filled with Auntie magic.

I see it now: the ivory tower in a snow globe with the sparkling flakes of Academic Auntie magic casting a beautiful spell on everyone and everything.

I hope we all get to attend the University of Auntie Magic.

# Journaling and Discussion Questions for "Academic Aunties"

1. How might education be different if Academic Auntieness were the default way of being in your own life or community? Describe examples from your own experiences in education, and in everyday life, that you think could be different, if infused with Auntie magic.

2. What is an example of Auntie magic that you've had the good fortune to witness or experience? Describe the circumstance. How did this example of Auntie magic impact you?

3. Name someone you know with whom you'd like to have tea, just to visit and enjoy one another's company. Why did you choose that person?

Extra credit: invite this person, if you can, to tea (or coffee) so that you can enjoy a visit together.

Bonus extra credit: make scones to go with the tea (or coffee). Even if your guest cannot attend your gathering, take some time to savor the sweet presence this person has in your life, and the world.

# The Perfect Yakama Auntie

I'm going to tell you about the Perfect Yakama Auntie.

She gathers all her own foods—roots, berries, fruits, and vegetables. She trades them for deer, elk, salmon, steelhead, and trout. She cooks and preserves them all with precision and grace, always having enough to give away whenever needed or inspired. No one has to ask. She just does it. She just *knows*.

She sews all her own clothes and makes wing dresses and ribbon shirts for her whole family, and large circle of friends and relatives, even for the children's dolls.

She can bead anything you want. She even beaded the steering wheel, seat belts, and exterior body of a Ford Pinto one time, cruising it in the Treaty Days

Parade in Toppenish; I think it's now on display in the Smithsonian. She does all this looking larger than life in her sky-high-tall Miss Indian World crown while she's taking a break from weaving her own impressive baskets.

She is fluent in her Indigenous language and all the related dialects of the region. She's listened and practiced and studied so diligently and thus can read and write all the dialects, too. People come from around the rez, the state, the Pacific Northwest, heck from around the *world* to hear her perfect pronunciation of some of our difficult words, like limlḵ'áx̱ and tl'tl'úmx̱.

She has great hair, always clean and neatly braided, no dandruff or oily streaks to be found.

She's won every Pow Wow contest category she's entered.

Her bookshelf is tightly crowded with softball and basketball trophies. It would collapse under the weight of all those awards, had it not been for all her barrel riding and bowling trophies on the floor, stacked precisely to prop it up, like the flying buttresses of Notre Dame Cathedral in Paris, where she once was invited to make her world-famous fry bread to serve as the communion hosts; they made an exception for the leavening agent because her fry bread is *that good.* We all got to fly first class to go over and witness that, and loved seeing the French folks and tourists licking powdered sugar off their hands as they strolled back to their pews. Amen, indeed!

Perfect Auntie always has at least two running cars, you know, one to use and one to lend whoever needs it. Keys are in it, just use it whenever. She pays for the insurance and gas, so no need to worry. Come by anytime, and it is ok if you dent the car; she'll get it fixed no problem.

Perfect Yakama Auntie attends Longhouse regularly and is a fabulous cook. Her food is so good even the Catholic priest attends Longhouse services, claiming to support interfaith community, but we all know he is just waiting for a piece of Auntie's perfectly baked huckleberry pie; yes, with a scoop of Auntie's homemade, hand churned vanilla ice cream. He loves those flecks of real vanilla beans. Oh! We forgot to put a dollop of her homemade whipped cream on top; she just finished whisking up a big bowl by hand. She can make a feast for 300 people without breaking a sweat!

Oh, did I say sweat? Yes, she builds and runs her own sweathouse, too, and has the endless time and patience and grace to welcome and guide eager apprentices, young people who want to know their culture but for a variety of reasons, both heartbreaking and pitiful, do not.

And so Perfect Yakama Auntie takes them under her wing, teaching them, until the young people inevitably lose interest, or can't cope with their latest heartbreak. Or car accident. Or best friend's suicide. Or the latest round of abuse in their home. Maybe another suspension from school. Perhaps there's a relapse into alcohol or drugs. And then the young people may lash out. Curse at Auntie. Or perhaps steal and pawn her beloved cedar basket that great-grandmother made.

Perfect Auntie witnesses this, strong and secure and patient as an oak tree; deep roots of prayer and discipline her Elders taught her keep her grounded. She has wisdom and love that make her unshakable in times of crisis.

At times like these, Perfect Auntie perhaps gets into one of her running cars, her cute rez dog jumping eagerly into the passenger seat, and they come looking for you, the wayward young person. Perhaps they find you staggering down the road by the big irrigation ditch. They come up the road, roll down the passenger window, and Auntie's dog gives you a kiss; his wet nose taking you momentarily out of your stupor and bringing you into the present.

Auntie says nothing. Just smiles gently, unjudging, with KC and the Sunshine Band playing softly in the background on KYNR. Auntie loves any song with "Boogie" in the title.

After a couple of moments, she asks, "How about we go get something to eat in town? Miner's? I'm kind of hungry for curly fries."

She waits patiently.

"Ok," you finally mumble, and get in.

Rez dog, aka incognito therapy dog, immediately begins his healing work, resting his chin on your knee and looking straight at you, with hope and love in his shiny brown eyes, kind of beaming it at you like some sort of Jedi dog.

As you ride with them up Lateral A, past one orchard and then the next, you can start to feel the effects of Jedi rez dog reflecting that hope and love back into your drunk and pitiful soul.

By the time you arrive to the Miner's parking lot you're feeling better, on your way to sober. You realize you're hungry for those orange-tinted curly fries. Auntie orders you both orange juice floats, too, because, "Vitamin C is probably good for us, eh?"

Afterwards, you go to the fabric store and you're allowed to pick out *any* fabric you like for a new outfit. You choose a red fabric that has blue flowers so small they look like polka dots.

"A stop at Dairy Queen on the way home?" Auntie asks you and Jedi rez dog when you're back in the car.

You and the dog both know she's already decided, and thus say nothing.

"Sure, why not." she answers herself.

After the last stop in town, Auntie says, "Tomorrow we'll go high up onto the ridge and dig pyaxí all morning. Then you can help me peel, and I'll make your new outfit. Won't it be nice to wear your outfit to the Longhouse?" It's not exactly a command, nor is it a request. It is a Perfect Auntie question/statement to which you know in your heart you cannot refuse.

Rez dog puts his chin on you again and wags his tail, urging you to go ahead and say yes.

"Ok," you agree, trying to sound reluctant. You rub Jedi rez dog's soft ears and begin to really remember what love and hope feel like. It's the perfect ending to an imperfect day.

None of us has THE Perfect Yakama Auntie, the mythical one woman who does everything flawlessly and can solve everyone's problems. But when we see *all* of the Aunties who surround us, each giving what they can of love and hope and time and patience, we can see that we *all* have access to the joy and wonder of Perfect Auntie, whose only reason to exist is to urge us on to love ourselves and the ones around us. When we see this, *we* are perfectly living our cultural teachings, by understanding the power of the collective to help us be outstanding individuals. To be strong yet gentle. Quick with a smile and fierce when needed. May we all nurture our inner Perfect Auntie.

Note: For readers wanting to practice Yakama Ichishkíin: limlḵ'áx̱ means poison oak, tl'tl'úmx̱ means red winged blackbird, and pyax̱í means bitterroot. To hear an almost-perfect-Yakama-Auntie, Tux̱ámshish Dr. Virginia Beavert, speak in our beautiful language, go to the website Tux̱ámshish and Dr. Sharon Hargus created; it is a great example of Academic Auntieness: http://depts.washington.edu/sahaptin/Sahdic.htm

# Journaling and Discussion Questions for "The Perfect Yakama Auntie"

1. What are some things that you cannot do, or have not accomplished, that you sometimes regret or feel badly about? Think of a specific example. Why do you think it makes you feel badly?

2. Take your bad feelings from the previous question, and place them aside. Now, think of some things that you are proud you can do or that you have accomplished. Why do you feel good about these things or accomplishments? We all get to choose our thoughts. What might the rest of your day be like if you focused more on these better thoughts, and less on the regretful thoughts?

3. One of the main points of "The Perfect Yakama Auntie" is that none of us are perfect. Describe what an Inner Perfect Auntie voice might tell you

about being kinder to yourself about your "failings" from Question 1 and celebrating your "accomplishments" from Question 2?

# Conclusion: Auntie Love Doesn't End

How do you end a book about Auntie-ing?

You don't. Not really.

The most powerful message I can tell you about Auntie Love is that it doesn't end.

Instead of concluding, let's go back to the beginning.

The Auntie Way is at its best when love, fun, and hope are ongoing.

What I've learned is that Auntie-ing means being a mere mortal trying to be the best and give the best that we can, even when we are flawed or lose our path on The Auntie Way, and also the profound ways that Aunties sweeten our lives, with treats and quilts, real and metaphorical.

Aunties show us how much they believe in us with gestures, glances, and words—pushing us forward to be our best selves.

Aunties listen to our questions and doubts and help us find our own answers, either through wise counsel or just as a patient listener.

Aunties are everywhere: the nurse at the IHS clinic, the aide in my kindergarten classroom, the librarian, the after-school club leader, coworkers, bosses, intern supervisors, coaches, and teachers. Recognized regardless of blood relation, because Aunties best distinguish themselves through demonstrating the care and concern of kin, with or without the sturdy branches of a family tree; Aunties can provide other trees, blossoming with hope and possibility.

As we reach the end of this book, I wish you much Auntie love. I wish you the kind of day and the kind of life that feels like you're surrounded by a parade of your favorite Aunties, all tossing you an endless supply of hope, love, kindness, fierceness, creativity, and care.

Let's all Auntie ourselves and each other.

Thank you for joining me; I look forward to seeing you on the path of The Auntie Way.

# About the Illustrator

Crystal L. Buck is a Native American artist and resides in Spokane, WA. She is an enrolled member of the Yakama Nation and grew up on the Yakama Indian Reservation. Her passion for drawing and painting evolved at a very young age. She gives credit to her amazing art teachers. They encouraged her and believed in her talent enough to enter her work in local shows throughout the years. Before completing high school, she participated in her 1st painting showcase where she met and networked with various artists. She sold her first piece in 1997. Upon graduating from college as an Exercise Specialist in 2003, she also received a minor in Art with a specialization in Painting from Fort Lewis College in Durango, CO. Most recently, her drawing was selected for the 2019-20 Washington State Indian Education Program logo. She is the mother of four beautiful children and loves spending time with her family. She enjoys participating in traditional gatherings and learning the Salish language with her kids. She's passionate about running, leading fitness dance classes, drawing and crafting. She is inspired by artistic creations that focus on her Native roots, modern art techniques, Zentangle, vibrant and various uses of colors, lines and patterns. One of her artistic dreams is to blend her love for hummingbirds and her individual style into a unique thematic masterpiece. You may contact Crystal by email: cry5tal_lea@yahoo.com

# About the Author

Michelle M. Jacob is an enrolled member of the Yakama Nation and has over 20 years of teaching experience, most currently at the University of Oregon where she is Professor of Indigenous Studies in the Department of Education Studies, and serves as Affiliated Faculty in the Department of Indigenous, Race, and Ethnic Studies, and Affiliated Faculty in the Environmental Studies Program. Michelle engages in scholarly and activist work that seeks to understand and work toward a holistic sense of health and well-being within Indigenous communities and among allies who wish to engage decolonization. Michelle's first two books, *Yakama Rising: Indigenous Cultural Revitalization, Activism, and Healing*, and, *Indian Pilgrims: Indigenous Journeys of Activism and Healing with Saint Kateri Tekakwitha*, were published by the University of Arizona Press. Dr. Jacob's third book, *On Indian Ground: A Return to Indigenous Knowledge-Generating Hope, Leadership and Sovereignty through Education in the Northwest*, was co-edited with Stephany RunningHawk Johnson, and published by Information Age Publishing. Michelle has numerous articles published in social science, education, and health science research journals, and grants from the U.S. Department of Education, the National Endowment for the Humanities, and the National Science Foundation. Her research areas of interest include: Indigenous methodologies, spirituality, health, education, Native feminisms, and decolonization. Dr. Jacob founded Anahuy Mentoring, LLC to support her vision of sharing Indigenous methodologies with a broad audience. Michelle is grateful to all her family and friends for their love and support, including her many blessed Aunties, who inspired *The Auntie Way* book.

Follow Michelle's blog at: www.auntieway.com

You may contact Michelle through the form on her website: www.anahuymentoring.com

# Author Acknowledgments

I am grateful to the fantastic Indigenous scholars who peer-reviewed this book manuscript: Leilani Sabzalian, Kirby Brown, Angie Morrill, Anthony Craig, Yvonne Sherwood, and Stephany RunningHawk Johnson. Deanna Chappell Belcher, Chris Andersen, and Theresa Jacob also offered valuable feedback on the manuscript. All feedback I received greatly strengthened this manuscript, and any weaknesses remain my own. I am grateful *The Auntie Way* is blessed with the beautiful artwork of Crystal Buck.

I've been fortunate to work with many supportive people who help me grow as a teacher, writer, and scholar—too many to name! I was inspired by fabulous colleagues at the places I've taught: University of Oregon, University of San Diego, MiraCosta College, Yakima Valley College, and Heritage University. I am grateful I was taught by several amazing faculty, staff, and peers at: UC Santa Barbara, CSU San Marcos, UC Irvine,

MiraCosta College, Seattle University, and Wapato Public Schools. I have wonderful colleagues at the University of Oregon College of Education, the Department of Education Studies, and my dear colleagues in our Sapsik'ʷałá Program. Thanks to the COE Finance team for their kindness and efficiency. The University of Oregon has a critical mass of outstanding Indigenous scholars and allies who are working on behalf of Tribal peoples; thanks to my colleagues in the Sapsik'ʷałá (Teacher) Education Program, Native American Studies Program, Northwest Indian Language Institute, and the Native Strategies Group. Thank you to the Whitefish Writers Circle and the many wonderful writers at Flathead Valley Community College.

Huge thanks to my family who have given me so much love and encouragement over the years: Dad, Mom, Uncle Jim, Roger, Gina, Garret, Hunter, Faith, Justin, Alicia, Quintic, Hazen, Blaise, Sealy, and my in-laws, who are a blessing!

This is an Auntie book, and I have *so many* Aunties I love and adore—too many to name! But special honor and love to three "Aunties" who've passed on, although their love endures: Elizabeth, Lucille, and Sue.

I'll end by thanking the world's greatest camping buddies, Chris and Anahuy. Áwna!

# About Anahuy Mentoring

Anahuy Mentoring is committed to engaging Indigenous methodologies to teach about the importance of Indigenous ways of knowing and being. *The Auntie Way* is published by Anahuy Mentoring, an independent Indigenous press that utilizes Indigenous cultural values in peer-review.

Learn more at:

http://www.anahuymentoring.com

Anahuy is the Yakama Ichishkíin word for black bear.

## ANAHUY MENTORING, LLC

EXCELLENCE IN INDIGENOUS METHODS

Made in the USA
Middletown, DE
05 September 2021

47627288R00073